In the Year 1955

by

Kerry Butters.

In the Year 1955.

Millennium: 2nd millennium

Centuries: 19th century – **20th century** – 21st century

Decades: 1920s 1930s 1940s – **1950s** – 1960s 1970s 1980s

Years: 1952 1953 1954 – **1955** – 1956 1957 1958

1955 (MCMLV) was a common year starting on Saturday (dominical letter B) of the Gregorian calendar, the 1955th year of the Common Era (CE) and *Anno Domini* (AD) designations, the 955th year of the 2nd millennium, the 55th year of the 20th century, and the 6th year of the 1950s decade.

January 7: Marian Anderson at the Met

Contents

Events

January

- January 2 – José Antonio Remón Cantera, president of Panama, is assassinated at a race track in Panama City.
- January 3 – José Ramón Guizado becomes president of Panama.
- January 7 – Marian Anderson is the first African-American singer to perform at the Metropolitan Opera in New York City.
- January 17 – USS *Nautilus*, the first nuclear-powered submarine, puts to sea for the first time, from Groton, Connecticut.
- January 18–January 20 – Battle of Yijiangshan Islands: The Chinese Communist People's Liberation Army seizes the islands from the Republic of China (Taiwan).
- January 22 – In the United States, The Pentagon announces a plan to develop intercontinental ballistic missiles (ICBMs) armed with nuclear weapons.
- January 23 – Sutton Coldfield rail crash kills 17 near Birmingham, England.

- January 25 – Presidium of the Supreme Soviet of the Soviet Union announces the end of the war between the USSR and Germany, which began during World War II in 1941.
- January 28 – United States Congress authorizes President Dwight D. Eisenhower to use force to protect Formosa from the People's Republic of China.

January 22: ICBM

February

- February 4 – "Baghdad Pact": Military treaty signed between Iraq and Turkey.
- February 9 – Apartheid in South Africa: 60,000 non-white residents of the Sophiatown suburb of Johannesburg are forcibly evicted.
- February 10 – The United States Seventh Fleet helps the Republic of China evacuate Chinese Nationalist army and residents from the Tachen Islands to Taiwan.
- February 12 – U.S. President Dwight D. Eisenhower sends the first U.S. advisors to South Vietnam.
- February 16 – Nearly 100 die in a fire at a home for the elderly in Yokohama, Japan.
- February 19 – Southeast Asia Treaty Organization established at a meeting in Bangkok.

- February 22 – In Chicago's Democratic primary, Mayor Martin H. Kennelly loses to the head of the Cook County Democratic Party, Richard J. Daley, 364,839 to 264,77.

March

- March – A young Jim Henson builds the first version of Kermit the Frog.
- March 2
  - Claudette Colvin, a fifteen-year-old African-American girl, refuses to give up her seat on a bus in Montgomery, Alabama, to a white woman after the driver demands it. She is carried off the bus backwards while being kicked and handcuffed and harassed on the way to the police station. She becomes a plaintiff in *Browder v. Gayle* (1956) which rules bus segregation to be unconstitutional.
  - Serious floods in Australia.
- March 5
  - WBBJ-TV signs on the air in the Jackson, Tennessee, with WDXI as its initial call-letters, to expanded American commercial television in mostly-rural areas.
  - Elvis Presley makes his television debut on "Louisiana Hayride" carried by KSLA-TV Shreveport (although audio recordings exists, there is no known video footage of this appearance).
- March 7 – The Broadway musical version of *Peter Pan*, which had opened in 1954 starring Mary Martin, is presented on television for the first time by NBC-TV with its original cast, as an installment of *Producers' Showcase*. It is also the first time that a stage musical is presented in its entirety on TV

almost exactly as it was performed on stage. This program gains the largest viewership of a TV special up to this time, and it becomes one of the first great TV family musical classics.

- March 17 – Richard Riot in Montreal: 6,000 people protest the suspension of French Canadian ice hockey star Maurice Richard of the Montreal Canadiens by the National Hockey League following a violent incident during a match.
- March 19 – KXTV signs on the air in Sacramento, California.
- March 20 – The movie adaptation of Evan Hunter's novel *Blackboard Jungle* premieres in the United States, featuring the famous single "Rock Around the Clock" by Bill Haley & His Comets. Teenagers jump from their seats to dance to the song.

April

- April 1 – EOKA A starts a terrorist campaign against British rule in the Crown colony of Cyprus.
- April 5
  - Winston Churchill resigns as Prime Minister of the United Kingdom due to ill-health at the age of 80.
  - Richard J. Daley defeats Robert Merrian to become Mayor of Chicago by a vote of 708,222 to 581,555.
- April 6 – Anthony Eden becomes Prime Minister of the United Kingdom.
- April 10 – in the NBA, the Syracuse Nationals defeat the Fort Wayne Pistons 92-91 in game seven to win the title.
- April 11 – The Taiwanese Kuomintang put a time-bomb on the airplane *Kashmir Princess*, killing 16 but failing to

assassinate the People's Republic of China leader, Zhou Enlai.

- April 12 – The Salk polio vaccine, having passed large-scale trials earlier in the United States, receives full approval by the Food and Drug Administration.
- April 14 – The Detroit Red Wings win the Stanley Cup for the 7th time in franchise history, but will not win again until 1997.

April 15: McDonald's

- April 15
    - Middle East Treaty Organization (MENTO).
    - Ray Kroc opens his first McDonald's in Des Plaines, Illinois.
- April 16 – Burma-Japanese peace treaty, signed in Rangoon on November 5, 1954, comes into effect, formally ending a state of war between the two countries that has not existed for a long time.
- April 17 – Imre Nagy, the communist Premier of Hungary, is ousted for being too moderate.
- April 18–April 24 – Asian-African Conference held in Bandung, Indonesia.

May

- May 1 – Warsaw Treaty on Friendship, Cooperation and Mutual Assistance signed (Warsaw Treaty Organization) (effective June 6).
- May 5 – West Germany becomes a sovereign country recognized by important Western foreign countries, such as France, the United Kingdom, Canada, and the United States.
- May 6 – Western European Union charter effective.
- May 9 – West Germany joins the North Atlantic Treaty Organization (NATO).
- May 11 – Japanese National Railways' ferry *Shiun Maru* sinks after collision with sister ship *Uko Maru* in thick fog off Takamatsu, Shikoku, in the Seto Inland Sea of Japan; 166 passengers (many children) and two crew are killed. This event is influential in plans to construct the Akashi Kaikyō Bridge (built 1986-98).
- May 12– New York's Third Avenue Elevated runs its last train between Chathem Square in Manhattan and East 149th Street in the Bronx, thus ending elevated train service in Manhattan.
- May 14 – Eight Communist Bloc countries, including the Soviet Union, sign a mutual defence treaty in Warsaw, Poland, that is called the Warsaw Pact. It will be dissolved in 1991.
- May 15 – Austrian State Treaty, which restores Austria's national sovereignty, is concluded between the four occupying powers following World War II (the United Kingdom, the United States, the Soviet Union, and France) and Austria, setting it up as a neutral country.

- May 25 – Joe Brown and George Band are the first to attain the summit of Kangchenjunga in the Himalayas, as part of a British team led by Charles Evans.

June

- June 7 – The television quiz program *The $64,000 Question* premieres on CBS-TV in the United States, with Hal March as the host.
- June 11 – Le Mans disaster: Eighty-three people are killed and at least 100 are injured after two race cars collide in the 1955 24 Hours of Le Mans.
- June 13 – Mir mine, the first diamond mine in the Soviet Union, is discovered.
- June 16 – *Lady and the Tramp*, the Walt Disney company's 15th animated film, premieres in Chicago.
- June 26 – Freedom Charter of the anti-apartheid South African Congress Alliance adopted at a Congress of the People in Kliptown.

July

July 7 – The New Zealand Special Air Service is formed.

- July 13 – Ruth Ellis is hanged for murder in London, becoming the last woman ever to be executed in the United Kingdom.
- July 17
  - The American Broadcasting Company broadcasts a sneak preview of Disneyland in Anaheim, California.

- Disneyland opens to the public in Anaheim, California.
- July 18
  - The first nuclear-generated electrical power is sold commercially, partially powering the town of Arco, Idaho.
  - The Illinois Governor, William Stratton, signs the "Loyalty Oath Act", passed by the State Legislature, which mandates all public employees take a loyalty oath to Illinois and the United States, or lose their jobs.
  - The first Geneva Summit meeting between the United States, the Soviet Union, the United Kingdom, and France begins. It ends on July 23.
- July 27 – El Al Flight 402 from Vienna, Austria to Tel Aviv via Istanbul is shot down over Bulgaria. All 58 passengers and crewmen aboard the Lockheed Constellation airplane are killed.
- July 28 – The first Interlingua Congress in Tours, France, leading to foundation of the Union Mundial pro Interlingua.

August

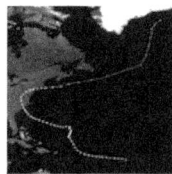

August 19: Hurricane Diane

- August 18
  - The First Sudanese Civil War begins.

- First meeting of the Organization of Central American States (*Organización de Estados Centroamericanos*, ODECA), in Antigua Guatemala.
- August 19 – Hurricane Diane hits the northeastern United States, killing over 200 people, and causing over $1.0 billion in damage.
- August 20 – Hundreds of people are killed in anti-French rioting in Morocco and Algeria.
- August 22 – Eleven schoolchildren are killed when their school bus is hit by a freight train in Spring City, Tennessee.
- August 25 – The last Soviet Army occupation forces leave Austria.
- August 26 – Release in India of Satyajit Ray's film *Pather Panchali*.
- August 27 – First edition of the *Guinness Book of Records* is published, in London.

September

September 18: Britain annexes Rockall

- September 2 – Under the guidance of Dr. Humphry Osmond, Christopher Mayhew ingests 400 mg of mescaline hydrochloride and allows himself to be filmed as part of a *Panorama* special for BBC TV in the U.K. that is never broadcast.
- September 6 – Istanbul pogrom: Istanbul's Greek minority is the target of a government-sponsored pogrom.
- September 10 – The long-running program *Gunsmoke* debuts on the CBS-TV network.
- September 14 – Pope Pius XII elevates many of the Apostolic vicariates in Africa to Metropolitan Archdioceses
- September 15 – Vladimir Nabokov's controversial novel *Lolita* is published in Paris by Olympia Press.
- September 18 – The United Kingdom formally annexes the uninhabited island of Rockall.
- September 19–September 21 – The President of Argentina, Juan Perón, is ousted in a military coup.
- September 19 – Hurricane Hilda kills about 200 people in Mexico.
- September 22 – Independent Commercial Television (ITV) begins broadcasting in the United Kingdom.
- September 24 – Dwight D. Eisenhower, President of the United States suffers a coronary thrombosis while on vacation in Denver, Colorado. Vice President Nixon serves as Acting President while Eisenhower recovers.
- September 30 – Actor James Dean is killed when his automobile collides with another car at a highway junction near Cholame, California.

October

- October 2 – *Alfred Hitchcock Presents* debuts on the CBS TV network in the United States.
- October 3 – *The Mickey Mouse Club* debuts on the ABC-TV network in the United States.
- October 4 – The Reverend Sun Myung Moon is released from prison in Seoul, South Korea.
- October 5 – Disneyland Hotel opens to the public in Anaheim, California.
- October 11 – 70-mm film for projection is introduced with the theatrical release of Rodgers and Hammerstein's musical film, *Oklahoma!*.
- October 14 – Organization of Central American States secretariat inaugurated.
- October 20 – Disc jockey Bill Randle of WERE (Cleveland) is the key presenter of a concert at Brooklyn High School (Ohio), featuring Pat Boone and Bill Haley & His Comets and opening with Elvis Presley, Elvis's first filmed performance, for a documentary on Randle titled *The Pied Piper of Cleveland*.
- October 26
  - After the last Allied troops have left Austria and following the provisions of the Austrian Independence Treaty, the country declares its permanent neutrality.
  - Ngô Đình Diệm proclaims Vietnam to be a republic with himself as its President (following the State of Vietnam referendum on October 23) and forms the Army of the Republic of Vietnam.

- October 27 – Film *Rebel Without a Cause*, starring James Dean, is released in the United States.
- October 29 – Soviet battleship *Novorossiysk* explodes at moorings in Sevastopol Bay, killing 608, the Soviet Union's worst naval disaster.

November

October 26: Austria free

- November 1
    - The Vietnam War begins between the South Vietnam Army and the North Vietnam Army in which the latter is allied with the Viet Cong.
    - A time bomb explodes in the cargo hold of United Airlines Flight 629, a Douglas DC-6B airliner flying above Longmont, Colorado, killing all 39 passengers and 5 crew members on board.
- November 3 – The Rimutaka Tunnel opens on the New Zealand Railways, at 5.46 mi (8.79 km) the longest in the Southern Hemisphere at this time.
- November 5 – Racial segregation is outlawed on trains and buses in interstate commerce in the United States.
- November 19 – C. Northcote Parkinson first propounds 'Parkinson's law', in *The Economist*.
- November 20 – Bo Diddley makes his television debut on Ed Sullivan's *Toast Of The Town* show for the CBS-TV network.

- November 23 – The Cocos Islands in the Indian Ocean are transferred from British to Australian control.
- November 26 – The British Governor of Cyprus declares a state of emergency on the island.

December

- December 1 – In Montgomery, Alabama, Rosa Parks refuses to obey bus driver James F. Blake's order that she give up her seat to make room for a white passenger and is arrested, leading to the Montgomery Bus Boycott.

December 14: Tappan Zee Bridge opens

- December 4 – The International Federation of Blood Donor Organizations was founded in Luxembourg.
- December 5
  - The American Federation of Labor and the Congress of Industrial Organizations merge to become the AFL–CIO.
  - The Montgomery Improvement Association is formed in Montgomery, Alabama, by Dr. Martin Luther King, Jr., and other Black ministers to coordinate a Black people's boycott of all city buses.
- December 9 – Adnan Menderes of DP forms the new government of Turkey (22nd government)

- December 14
  - The Tappan Zee Bridge over the Hudson River in New York State opens to traffic.
  - Albania, Austria, Bulgaria, Cambodia, Finland, Hungary, Ireland, Italy, Jordan, Laos, Libya, Nepal, Portugal, Romania, Spain, and Sri Lanka join the United Nations simultaneously, after several years of moratorium on admitting new members that began during the Korean War.
- December 20 – Cardiff is declared by the British Government as the capital of Wales.
- December 22 – American cytogeneticist Joe Hin Tjio discovers the correct number of human chromosomes, forty-six.
- December 31 – General Motors becomes the first American corporation to make a profit of over one billion dollars in one year.

Date unknown

- The Strömsund Bridge in Sweden is completed, being the first significant cable-stayed bridge of the modern era.[1]

World population

- World population: 2,755,823,000
  - Africa: 246,746,000
  - Asia: 1,541,947,000
  - Europe: 575,184,000
  - South America: 190,797,000
  - North America: 186,884,000
  - Oceania: 14,265,000

Births

January

Rowan Atkinson

J. K. Simmons

Kevin Costner

Simon Rattle

John G. Roberts

Nicolas Sarkozy

- January 1
  - Mario Andreacchio, Australian film director
  - Mary Beard, English classicist
  - Precious, Canadian professional wrestling valet
- January 2 – Vivien Savage, French singer
- January 5 – Mamata Banerjee, Indian politician, Chief Minister of West Bengal
- January 6 – Rowan Atkinson, English comedian and actor
- January 9 – J. K. Simmons, American actor
- January 10 – Michael Schenker, German guitarist (Scorpions, UFO, Michael Schenker Group)
- January 13
  - Ran Ito, Japanese actress
  - Paul Kelly, Australian musician
  - Jay McInerney, American writer

- January 15
  - Andreas Gursky, German photographer
  - Mayumi Tanaka, Japanese voice actress
- January 17
  - Steve Earle, American musician
  - Mami Koyama, Japanese voice actress
- January 18 – Kevin Costner, American actor, producer and director
- January 19 – Sir Simon Rattle, English orchestral conductor
- January 20
  - Joe Doherty, Provisional Irish Republican Army member
  - Hiromi Ōta, Japanese singer
- January 21 – Jeff Koons, American artist
- January 22 – Keiko Takahashi, Japanese actress
- January 25 – Petra Gerster, German television presenter and newscaster
- January 26
  - Björn Andrésen, Swedish actor
  - Eddie Van Halen, Dutch-born American rock musician (Van Halen)
- January 27
  - John G. Roberts, Jr., Chief Justice of the United States
  - Alexander Stuart, British-born author
- January 28
  - Vinod Khosla, Indian-born American venture capitalist
  - Nicolas Sarkozy, President of France
  - George Tokoro, Japanese TV personality and singer-songwriter

- January 29
  - Eddie Jordan, American basketball player and head coach
  - Femi Pedro, Deputy Governor of Lagos State, Nigeria

February

Kelsey Grammer

Steve Jobs

- February 1 – Hans Werner Olm, German television and film comedian
- February 2 – Leszek Engelking, Polish poet, writer and translator
- February 3 – Kirsty Wark, Scottish television presenter
- February 6 – Michael Pollan, American journalist
- February 6 – Irinej Dobrijević, American-born Serbian Bishop of Australia and New Zealand
- February 7 – Miguel Ferrer, American actor
- February 8
  - John Grisham, American novelist

- Xu Bing, Chinese artist
- February 9
  - Charles Shaughnessy, English-born actor
  - Jim J. Bullock, American actor and comedian
- February 10
  - Chris Adams, English wrestler and judoka (d. 2001)
  - Pablo Borges Delgado, Cuban artist
  - Greg Norman, Australian golfer
- February 12 – Ai Satō, Japanese voice actress
- February 13 – Akiko Yano, Japanese singer-songwriter
- February 15
  - Janice Dickinson, American model, photographer, author and talent agent
  - Christopher McDonald, American actor
- February 17 – Mo Yan, Chinese writer
- February 19 – Jeff Daniels, American actor
- February 21 – Kelsey Grammer, American actor and comedian
- February 23
  - Howard Jones, English pop keyboardist and singer-songwriter
  - Flip Saunders, American basketball coach (d. 2015)
- February 24
  - Steve Jobs, American businessman and founder of Apple Inc. (d. 2011)
  - Alain Prost, French race car driver

March

Penn Jillette

Nina Hagen

Gary Sinise

Bruce Willis

Angus Young

- March 1 – Sir Timothy Laurence, English admiral and second husband of Anne, Princess Royal
- March 2
  - Shoko Asahara, Japanese cult leader (Aum Shinrikyo)
  - Jay Osmond, American pop singer
- March 3 – Kent Derricott, Canadian TV personality in Japan
- March 4 – Dominique Pinon, French actor
- March 5
  - Julien Dray, French politician
  - Penn Jillette, American magician and comedian (Penn & Teller)
- March 6
  - Cyprien Ntaryamira, Burundian politician, 5th President of Burundi (d. 1994)
  - Alberta Watson, Canadian actress (d. 2015)
- March 7 – Tommy Kramer, American football player
- March 8 – Don Ashby, Canadian ice hockey player (d. 1981)
- March 9
  - Ornella Muti, Italian actress
  - Franco Uncini, Italian motorcycle racer
- March 10
  - Yousra, Egyptian actress and singer
  - Marianne Rosenberg, German singer
- March 11 – Nina Hagen, German pop singer

- March 13
  - Bruno Conti, Italian football player
  - Glenne Headly, American actress of film, stage and television
- March 15
  - Robert Kabbas, Egyptian-born Australian weightlifter
  - Dee Snider, American rock singer (Twisted Sister)
- March 16
  - Bruno Barreto, Brazilian film director
  - Jiro Watanabe, Japanese boxer
- March 17 – Gary Sinise, American actor, producer and director
- March 18
  - Guillermo Dávila, Venezuelan actor and singer
  - Dwayne Murphy, American baseball player
- March 19
  - Bruce Willis, American actor
  - Simon Yam, Hong Kong actor
  - Pino Daniele, Italian music artist (d. 2015)
- March 20 – Mariya Takeuchi, Japanese singer-songwriter
- March 21 – Philippe Troussier, French football coach
- March 22
  - Lena Olin, Swedish actress
  - Pete Sessions, American politician
  - Valdis Zatlers, president of Latvia
- March 23 – Moses Malone, American basketball player (d. 2015)
- March 24
  - Celâl Şengör, Turkish geologist
  - Kim Johnston Ulrich, American actress
- March 26 – Danny Arndt, Canadian ice hockey player

- March 27 – Mariano Rajoy, Prime Minister of Spain
- March 28
  - John Alderdice, Irish politician
  - Reba McEntire, American country singer and actress
- March 29
  - Earl Campbell, American football player
  - Brendan Gleeson, Irish actor
  - Marina Sirtis, English-born actress
- March 31 – Angus Young, Scottish-born Australian rock guitarist

April

Henri, Grand Duke of Luxembourg

Kate Mulgrew

- April 3
  - Michael Burleigh, British historian
  - Mick Mars, American rock guitarist (Mötley Crüe)
- April 5
  - Janice Long, English radio disc jockey

- Akira Toriyama, Japanese manga artist
- April 6 – Michael Rooker, American actor
- April 7
  - Grace Hightower, American philanthropist, actress and singer
  - Gregg Jarrett, American lawyer turned journalist
  - Akira Nishino, Japanese soccer player and manager
  - Werner Stocker, German actor (d. 1993)
- April 8
  - Kane Hodder, American actor
  - Barbara Kingsolver, American fiction writer
- April 9 – Kate Heyhoe, American food writer
- April 11 – Kevin Brady, American politician
- April 13
  - Steve Camp, American Christian musician
  - Hideki Saijo, Japanese singer and actor
- April 15 – Dodi Fayed, Egyptian businessman (d. 1997)
- April 16
  - Henri, Grand Duke of Luxembourg
  - DJ Kool Herc, Jamaican American DJ
- April 17 – Rob Bolland, Dutch musician, songwriter and music producer (Bolland & Bolland)
- April 18 – Bobby Castillo, American baseball player (d. 2014)
- April 21
  - Ebiet G. Ade, Indonesian singer and songwriter
  - Toninho Cerezo, Brazilian footballer and coach
- April 23
  - Judy Davis, Australian actress
  - Fumi Hirano, Japanese voice actress and essayist
  - Tony Miles, English chess player (d. 2001)
- April 24 – John de Mol, Dutch media tycoon

- April 25
  - John Nunn, English chess player and mathematician
  - Parviz Parastui, Iranian actor
- April 26 – Chen Daoming, Chinese actor
- April 27
  - James Risen, American Pulitzer Prize-winning investigative reporter and author
  - Eric Schmidt, American software engineer and businessman, former CEO of Google (2001-2011)
- April 28 – Eddie Jobson, English musician
- April 29
  - Richard Epcar, American voice actor
  - Kate Mulgrew, American actress
  - Yūko Tanaka, Japanese actress
- April 30 – Zlatko Topčić, Bosnian writer and screenwriter

May

Tom Bergeron

Meles Zenawi

Bill Paxton

James Gosling

- May 1
  - Ray Buttigieg, Maltese composer and poet
  - Nick Feldman, English musician (Wang Chung)
- May 2
  - Willie Miller, Scottish footballer
  - Donatella Versace, Italian designer
  - Dave Winer, American software pioneer
- May 3 – David Hookes, Australian cricketer (d. 2004)
- May 4
  - Avram Grant, Israeli football manager
  - Robert Ellis Orrall, American singer
- May 6 – Tom Bergeron, American television host
- May 7 – Mayra Alejandra, Venezuelan actress (d. 2014)
- May 8 – Meles Zenawi, Prime Minister of Ethiopia (d. 2012)
- May 9 – Anne Sofie von Otter, Swedish mezzo-soprano
- May 10
  - Chris Berman, American sports broadcaster

- o Mark David Chapman, American murderer of musician John Lennon
- May 14
  - o Robert Tapert, American TV producer
- May 16
  - o Olga Korbut, Russian gymnast
  - o Olli Kortekangas, Finnish composer
  - o Jack Morris, American baseball player
  - o Hazel O'Connor, English singer-songwriter and actress
  - o Debra Winger, American actress
- May 17 – Bill Paxton, American actor
- May 18 – Chow Yun-fat, Hong Kong actor
- May 19
  - o Mark Staff Brandl, American and Swiss artist and art historian
  - o James Gosling, Canadian software engineer
  - o Th. Emil Homerin, American theologian
- May 20
  - o Diego Abatantuono, Italian actor
  - o Zbigniew Preisner, Polish film composer
- May 22
  - o Chalmers "Spanky" Alford, American jazz guitarist (d. 2008)
  - o Dale Winton, English radio DJ and television presenter
- May 24
  - o Rosanne Cash, American entertainer
  - o Rumiko Ukai, Japanese voice actress
- May 25
  - o Suguru Egawa, Japanese baseball player
  - o Connie Sellecca, American actress

- May 26
  - Doris Dörrie, German actress and screenplay writer
  - Masaharu Morimoto, Japanese chef
- May 29 – Mike Porcaro, American bass guitarist (d. 2015)
- May 30
  - Nakamura Kanzaburō XVIII, Japanese Kabuki actor
  - Colm Tóibín. Irish novelist
- May 31
  - Tommy Emmanuel, Australian guitarist
  - Susie Essman, American actress
  - Lynne Truss, English writer

June

Laurie Metcalf

Michel Platini

Tim Berners-Lee

- June 1 – Chiyonofuji Mitsugu, Japanese sumo wrestler (58th Yokozuna grand champion)
- June 2 – Dana Carvey, American actor and comedian
- June 5 – Fernando Borrego Linares, Cuban singer and songwriter (aka Polo Montañez)
- June 6
  - Sandra Bernhard, American comedian, actress, author and singer
  - Chris Nyman, American baseball player
  - Sam Simon, American filmmaker (d. 2015)
- June 7 – Tim Richmond, American race car driver (d. 1989)
- June 8
  - Tim Berners-Lee, English computer scientist and inventor
  - Griffin Dunne, American actor and director
- June 10
  - Floyd Bannister, American baseball player
  - Andrew Stevens, American actor, producer and director
- June 11 – Yuriy Sedykh, Ukrainian hammer thrower
- June 14
  - Kim Lankford, American actress, businesswoman and horse wrangler
  - Paul O'Grady (also known as "Lily Savage"), English talk show host and comedian
- June 15 – Polly Draper, American actress, screenwriter, playwright, producer and director
- June 16 – Laurie Metcalf, American actress
- June 18 – Sandy Allen, American, world's tallest woman (d. 2008)
- June 20 – Tor Nørretranders, Danish author

- June 21
  - Aloysius Amwano, Nauruan politician
  - Tim Bray, Canadian computer programmer
  - Jean-Pierre Mader, French singer-songwriter
  - Leigh McCloskey, American actor
  - Michel Platini, French retired football player and President of UEFA
- June 22 – Glenn Danzig, American rock singer (The Misfits, Samhain, Danzig)
- June 23 – Alan J. Gow, Australian-born British motorsport executive
- June 24 – Gurumayi Chidvilasananda, Indian head of Siddha Yoga
- June 25 – Mike McShane, American actor, comedian and voice actor
- June 26 – Yoko Gushiken, Japanese boxer
- June 27
  - Isabelle Adjani, French actress
  - Brad Diller, American cartoonist

July

Lindsey Graham

Willem Dafoe

- July 1
  - Sanma Akashiya, Japanese comedian and actor
  - Nikolai Demidenko, Russian classical pianist
  - Li Keqiang, Premier of the People's Republic of China
  - Lisa Scottoline, American novelist
- July 2 – Stephen Walt, American political scientist
- July 3
  - John Cramer, American game show announcer
  - Matt Keough, American baseball player
- July 5
  - Sebastian Barry, Irish playwright, novelist and poet
  - Henry Lee Summer, American singer
- July 7 – Rolf Saxon, American actor
- July 8 – Mihaela Mitrache, Romanian actress
- July 9
  - Lindsey Graham, American politician, U.S. Senator (R-Sc.)
  - Fred Norris, American radio personality
  - Jimmy Smits, American actor
- July 11 – Balaji Sadasivan, Singaporean politician and neurosurgeon
- July 18 – Bernd Fasching, Austrian painter and sculptor
-

- July 21
  - Marcelo Bielsa, Argentine football player and manager
  - Howie Epstein, American musician and producer (d. 2003)
  - Béla Tarr, Hungarian film director
- July 22
  - Willem Dafoe, American actor
  - Asif Ali Zardari, Pakistani politician
- July 25 – Iman, Somalian model
- July 26 – Michele Pillar, American Christian musician
- July 27 – Allan Border, Australian cricketer
- July 31 – Jakie Quartz, French singer

August

Billy Bob Thornton

Daryl

Mike Huckabee

- August 2 – Caleb Carr, American writer
- August 3 – Roger Gifford, Lord Mayor of London 2013
- August 4
  - Gerrie Coetzee, South African boxer
  - Billy Bob Thornton, American actor, director and screenwriter
- August 6
  - Gordon J. Brand, English golfer
  - Ron Davis, American baseball player
- August 7
  - Vladimir Sorokin, Russian writer
  - Wayne Knight, American actor and comedian
- August 8 – Diddú (Sigrún Hjálmtýsdóttir), Icelandic soprano and songwriter
- August 9 – Doug Williams, American football quarterback
- August 10 – Mel Tiangco, Philippine television host and newscaster 24 Oras
- August 12
  - Heintje Simons, Dutch singer and actor
  - Gish Jen, American fiction writer
- August 13 – Daryl, American magician
- August 14 – Gillian Taylforth, English television actress
- August 17 – Richard Hilton, American businessman
-

- August 19
  - Peter Gallagher, American actor
  - Terry Harper, American baseball player
- August 20 – Agnes Chan, Hong Kong-born TV personality in Japan
- August 22
  - Chiranjeevi, Indian actor
  - Gordon Liu, Chinese actor
- August 24 – Mike Huckabee, American politician, former Governor and 2008 Presidential candidate
- August 27
  - Laura Fygi, Dutch singer
  - Sergey Khlebnikov, Soviet speed skater (d. 1999)
- August 30 –
  - Mayumi Muroyama, Japanese manga artist
  - Helge Schneider, comedian, jazz musician and multi-instrumentalist, author, film and theatre director
- August 31
  - Olek Krupa, Polish actor
  - Edwin Moses, American athlete

September

Zucchero Fornaciari

- September 1
  - Billy Blanks, American martial artist; inventor of the Tae Bo exercise program
  - Bruce Foxton, English musician
- September 2
  - Robert Duncan, American astrophysicist
  - Claus Kleber, German television journalist
  - Natalya Petrusyova, Soviet speed skater
  - Michelle Yim, Hong Kong actress
- September 4 – Hiroshi Izawa, Japanese actor
- September 6 – Raymond Benson, American author
- September 7 – Efim Zelmanov, Russian mathematician
- September 9 – John Kricfalusi, Canadian cartoonist
- September 12 – Peter Scolari, American actor and comedian
- September 15
  - Željka Antunović, Croatian politician
  - Brendan O'Carroll, Irish actor and comedian
  - Bruce Reitherman, American filmmaker and voice actor
  - Renzo Rosso, Italian clothing designer
- September 16
  - Janet Ellis, British children's TV presenter
  - Robin Yount, American baseball player
- September 17 – Charles Martinet, American voice-actor
- September 19 – Richard Burmer, American composer, sound designer and musician (d. 2006)
- September 21 – Richard Hieb, American astronaut
- September 24 – Shinbo Nomura, Japanese manga artist
- September 25
  - Karl-Heinz Rummenigge, German football player
  - Zucchero Fornaciari, Italian singer-songwriter
- September 28 – Stéphane Dion, Canadian politician

October

Bill Gates

- October 2 – Philip Oakey, English rock musician (The Human League)
- October 5
    - Jean-Jacques Lafon, French singer-songwriter
    - Caroline Loeb, French singer and actress
- October 7 – Yo-Yo Ma, French-born Chinese American cellist
- October 8
    - Bill Elliott, American racing driver
    - Darrell Hammond, Comedian (SNL)
- October 13 – Sergei Shepelev, Russian ice hockey player
- October 15
    - James B. Aguayo-Martel, Mexican-born physician, surgeon, scientist and inventor
    - Kulbir Bhaura, Indian-born British field hockey player
    - Tanya Roberts, American actress
    - Emily Yoffe, American journalist and advice columnist
- October 18
    - Hiromi Go, Japanese singer
    - Timmy Mallett, English television presenter
- October 19 – LaSalle Ishii, Japanese television personality
- October 21
    - Yasukazu Hamada, Japanese politician

- ○ Rich Mullins, American Christian musician (d. 1997)
- October 24
    - ○ Karen Austin, American actress
    - ○ Katherine Knight, Australian mariticide
- October 25 – Glynis Barber, South African-born British actress
- October 28
    - ○ Bill Gates, American businessman and co-founder of Microsoft
    - ○ Indra Nooyi, Indian business executive
- October 29
    - ○ Kevin DuBrow, American rock singer (d. 2007)
    - ○ Roger O'Donnell, English rock keyboardist
    - ○ Etsuko Shihomi, Japanese actress
- October 30 – Jeremy Black, British historian
- October 31 – Eduardo V. Manalo, 3rd Executive Minister (*Tagapamahalang Pangkalahatan*) of the *Iglesia ni Cristo* (Church of Christ)

November

Kris Jenner

Roland Emmerich

Whoopi Goldberg

Bill Nye

Howie Mandel

Billy Idol

- November 2 – Chris Burnett, American saxophone player, composer, veteran of US military jazz bands and band leader
- November 3
    - Teresa De Sio, Italian singer-songwriter
    - Phil Simms, American football player
    - Yukihiko Tsutsumi, Japanese film director
- November 4 – Moulana Ghousavi Shah, Sufi teacher and author, Secretary General of The Conference of World Religions
- November 4 – Matti Vanhanen, Prime Minister of Finland
- November 5
    - Pedro Brieger, Argentine journalist and sociologist.
    - Kris Jenner, American television personality
    - Karan Thapar, Indian journalist, political analyst and commentator
- November 6 – Maria Shriver, American television journalist, host; First Lady of California
- November 7 – Detlef Ultsch, German judo athlete
- November 9 – Karen Dotrice, Guernsey-born child actress
- November 10 – Roland Emmerich, German film director
- November 11 – Jigme Singye Wangchuck, King of Bhutan
- November 13 – Whoopi Goldberg, American actress and comedian

- November 14 – Koichi Nakano, Japanese bicycle racer
- November 17 – Peter Cox, English singer-songwriter (Go West)
- November 19 – Dianne de Leeuw, Dutch figure skater
- November 20 – Ray Ozzie, American computer programmer
- November 21
    - Kyle Gann, American composer and music critic
    - Cedric Maxwell, American basketball player
- November 22 – George Alagiah, Ceylonese-born British newsreader, journalist and television news presenter
- November 23
    - Steven Brust, American author
    - Ludovico Einaudi, Italian pianist and composer
- November 24 – Sir Ian Botham, English cricketer
- November 25 – Bruno Tonioli, film, music video and theater choreographer
- November 26 – Tracy Hickman, American author
- November 27 – Bill Nye, American science presenter and public television host
- November 28 – Alessandro Altobelli, Italian football player
- November 29 – Howie Mandel, Canadian actor and game show host
- November 30
    - Michael Beschloss, American historian
    - Kevin Conroy, American voice actor
    - Billy Idol, born William Broad, English rock singer

December

Jane Kaczmarek

- December 3
  - Melody Anderson, Canadian actress and social worker
  - Steven Culp, American actor
- December 4 – Maurizio Bianchi, Italian musician
- December 7 – Priscilla Barnes, American actress
- December 8
  - Ian Greig, South African-born English cricketer
  - Martin Semmelrogge, German actor
- December 9 – Asashio Tarō IV, Japanese sumo wrestler
- December 12 – Gianna Angelopoulos-Daskalaki, Greek politician and businesswoman
- December 16
  - Chiharu Matsuyama, Japanese singer-songwriter
  - Rob Levin, American founder of the freenode IRC network (d. 2006)
- December 17 – Brad Davis, American basketball player
- December 21 – Jane Kaczmarek, American actress
- December 23
  - Keith Comstock, American baseball player
  - Carol Ann Duffy, Scottish poet
  -

- December 24
  - Mizuho Fukushima, Japanese politician
  - Clarence Gilyard, American actor and college professor
- December 27 – Barbara Olson, American television commentator (d. 2001)
- December 28 – Liu Xiaobo, Chinese literary critic and human rights activist
- December 31 – Jim Tracy, American baseball player

Date unknown

- Mark Marderosian, American cartoonist

Deaths

January

- January 1 – Shanti Swaroop Bhatnagar, Indian scientist (b. 1894)
- January 2 – José Antonio Remón Cantera, President of Panama (assassinated) (b. 1908)
- January 6 – Yevgeny Tarle, Soviet historian (b. 1874)
- January 11 – Rodolfo Graziani, Italian general (b. 1882)
- January 15
  - Johannes Baader, German artist (b. 1875)
  - Yves Tanguy, French painter (b. 1900)
- January 18 – August Duesenberg, German-born American automobile manufacturer (b. 1879)
- January 20 – Robert P. T. Coffin, American poet (b. 1892)
- January 21 – Archie Hahn, American athlete (b. 1880)

- January 24 – Ira Hayes, U.S. Marine flag raiser on Iwo Jima (b. 1923)
- January 29 – Hans Hedtoft, Prime Minister of Denmark (b. 1903)
- January 31 – John Mott, American YMCA leader, recipient of the Nobel Peace Prize (b. 1865)

February

- February 11 – Ona Munson, American actress (b. 1903)
- February 12
  - Thomas J. Moore, Irish-American film actor (b. 1883)
  - S. Z. Sakall, Hungarian actor (b. 1883)
- February 20 – Oswald Avery, American physician and medical researcher (b. 1877)
- February 23 – Paul Claudel, French poet, dramatist, and diplomat (b. 1868)
- February 27 – Trixie Friganza, American actress (b. 1870)

March

Matthew Henson

Sir Alexander Fleming

- March 3 – Katharine Drexel, American Roman Catholic saint (b. 1858)
- March 8 – William C. deMille, American screenwriter and director (b. 1878)
- March 9 – Matthew Henson, American explorer (b. 1866)
- March 11 – Sir Alexander Fleming, Scottish scientist, recipient of the Nobel Prize in Physiology or Medicine (b. 1881)
- March 12 – Charlie Parker, American saxophonist (b. 1920)
- March 16 – Nicolas de Staël, Russian painter (b. 1914)
- March 23 – Artur da Silva Bernardes, President of Brazil (b. 1875)
- March 30 – Ylla, Hungarian photographer (b. 1911) (jeep accident)

April

Albert Einstein

- April 7 – Theda Bara, American film actress (b. 1885)
- April 10 – Pierre Teilhard de Chardin, French Jesuit priest, philosopher, paleontologist and geologist (b. 1881)
- April 11 – Clifton Sprague, American admiral (b. 1896)
- April 18 – Albert Einstein, German-born physicist, Nobel Prize laureate (b. 1879)
- April 25 – Constance Collier, stage and screen actress; acting coach (b. 1878)

May

- May 4
  - Louis Charles Breguet, French aircraft designer and builder and early aviation pioneer (b. 1880)
  - George Enescu, Romanian composer (b. 1881)
- May 10
  - Tommy Burns, American boxer (b. 1881)
  - John Radecki, Australian stained-glass artist (b. 1865)
- May 11 – Gilbert Jessop, English cricketer (b. 1874)
- May 14
  - Charles Pelot Summerall, American general (b. 1867)
  - Anwar Wagdi, Egyptian actor and filmmaker (b. 1904)
- May 16 – James Agee, American writer (b. 1909)
- May 17 – Owen Roberts, American Supreme Court Justice (b. 1875)
- May 18 – Mary McLeod Bethune, American educator (b. 1875)
- May 22 – Richard "Skeets" Gallagher, American actor (b. 1891)
- May 26 – Alberto Ascari, Italian race-car driver (b. 1918)
- May 30 – Bill Vukovich, American race-car driver (b. 1918)

June

Pattillo Higgins

- June 5
  - Pattillo Higgins, American oil pioneer and businessman (b. 1863)
  - Herbert Stanley, Governor of Northern Rhodesia, Ceylon and Southern Rhodesia (b. 1872)
- June 11 – Walter Hampden, American actor (b. 1879)
- June 17 – Carlyle Blackwell, American actor (b. 1884)
- June 19 – Adrienne Monnier, French poet (b. 1892)
- June 26 – Engelbert Zaschka, German helicopter pioneer (b. 1895)

July

- July 3 – Beatrice Chase, English writer (b. 1874)
- July 13
  - Ruth Ellis, Welsh-born murderer, last woman to be executed in the United Kingdom (b. 1926)
  - Stanley Price, American film and television actor (b. 1892)
- July 23 – Cordell Hull, United States Secretary of State, recipient of the Nobel Peace Prize (b. 1871)
- July 20 – Calouste Gulbenkian, Armenian businessman and philanthropist (b. 1869)
- July 31 – Robert Francis, American actor (b. 1930)

August

Carmen Miranda

Thomas Mann

- August 2
  - Rupprecht, Crown Prince of Bavaria, Bavarian military leader and last Bavarian crown prince (b. 1869)
  - Wallace Stevens, American poet (b. 1879)
- August 5 – Carmen Miranda, Portuguese Brazilian singer and actress (b. 1909)
- August 8 – Grace Hartman, American actress (b. 1907)
- August 12
  - Thomas Mann, German novelist, Nobel Prize laureate (b. 1875)
  - James B. Sumner, American chemist, Nobel Prize laureate (b. 1887)
- August 13 – Florence Easton, English-born operatic soprano (b. 1882)
- August 17 – Fernand Léger, French painter and sculptor (b. 1881)
- August 27 – Augusto Turati, Italian fascist politician (b. 1888)
- August 28 – Emmett Till, American murder victim (b. 1941)

September

James Dean

- September 1 – Philip Loeb, American actor (b. 1891)
- September 20 – Robert Riskin, American screenwriter (b. 1897)
- September 23 – Martha Norelius, American Olympic swimmer (b. 1908)
- September 24 – Ib Schønberg, Danish actor (b. 1902)
- September 30
  - Michael Chekhov, Russian actor and writer (b. 1891)
  - James Dean, American actor (b. 1931)

October

José Ortega y Gasset

- October 1 – Charles Christie, American film studio owner (b. 1880)
- October 8 – Iry LeJeune, Cajun musician (b. 1928)
-

- October 9
  - Theodor Innitzer, Cardinal Archbishop of Vienna (b. 1875)
  - Alice Joyce, American actress (b. 1890)
- October 13 – Manuel Ávila Camacho, 45th President of Mexico (b. 1897)
- October 18 – José Ortega y Gasset, Spanish philosopher (b. 1883)
- October 19 – John Hodiak, American actor (b. 1914)
- October 31 – William Woodward, Jr., American banker and horse breeder, shot to death by his wife (b. 1920)

November

Alfréd Hajós

- November 1 – Dale Carnegie, American writer and lecturer (b. 1888)
- November 4 – Cy Young, American baseball player (Cleveland Spiders) and a member of the MLB Hall of Fame (b. 1867)
- November 5 – Maurice Utrillo, French artist (b. 1882)
- November 7 – Tom Powers, American actor (b. 1890)
- November 11 – Jerry Ross, American lyricist and composer (b. 1926)

- November 12 – Alfréd Hajós, Hungarian swimmer and architect (b. 1878)
- November 13 – Moshe Pessach, chief rabbi of Volos (b. 1869)
- November 14 – Robert E. Sherwood, American playwright (b. 1896)
- November 15 – Lloyd Bacon, American actor and director (b. 1889)
- November 17 – Helmuth Weidling, German general (b. 1891)
- November 22 – Shemp Howard, American actor and comedian (The Three Stooges) (b. 1895)
- November 27 – Arthur Honegger, French-born Swiss composer (b. 1892)

December

- December 1 – Chief Thundercloud, American character actor (b. 1899)
- December 6
  - George Platt Lynes, American photographer (b. 1907)
  - Honus Wagner, American baseball player (Pittsburgh Pirates) and a member of the MLB Hall of Fame (b. 1874)
- December 13 – Egas Moniz, Portuguese neurologist, recipient of the Nobel Prize in Physiology or Medicine (b. 1874)
- December 21 – Garegin Nzhdeh, Armenian statesman (b. 1886)
- December 22 – Otto Eppers, American cartoonist (b. 1893)
- December 25
  - Elizabeth Harrison, daughter of President Benjamin Harrison and Mary Dimmick Harrison (b. 1897)

- Thomas J. Preston, Jr., professor of Archeology at Princeton University; second husband of Frances Cleveland, widow of President Grover Cleveland (b. 1862)
- December 27 – Alfred Francis Blakeney Carpenter, English soldier (b. 1881)

Nobel Prizes

- Physics – Willis Eugene Lamb and Polykarp Kusch
- Chemistry – Vincent du Vigneaud
- Physiology or Medicine – Axel Hugo Theodor Theorell
- Literature – Halldór Kiljan Laxness
- Peace – not awarded

In the News

Hurricane Diane hits the northeast United States, killing 200 and causing over $1 billion in damage.

The first Commercial TV Station with advertisements starts in London, England.

The USS Nautilus becomes the first operational nuclear powered submarine when it casts off on its first true voyage in January.

Jonas Salk's polio vaccine is declared safe and effective in April.

British Newspapers Not Printed for 1 month due to strike in Fleet Street By Maintenance Workers.

Clement Attlee who oversaw the creation of the British Welfare System resigns as leader of the Labour Party.

Princess Margaret announces she will not marry divorced Group Captain Peter Townsend.

Ruth Ellis the last woman in England to be executed is hung at Holloway Prison.

The United States begins its involvement in the Vietnam conflict.

Emmett Till, a black fourteen year old teenager is murdered for not showing respect to a white woman in Money, Miss.

West Germany Joins NATO.

Fish Fingers are marketed by Bird's Eye.

Popular Films - Oklahoma, The Quatermass Xperiment, Rebel without a Cause, To Catch A Thief, The Quatermass Xperiment, The seven year itch.

www.ingramcontent.com/pod-product-compliance
Lightning Source LLC
Chambersburg PA
CBHW060647290526
45793CB00001B/438